From

Fear

to

Faith

The Shift that Changed My Life

By: Brittney L. Kendle

Copyright © 2021 Brittney L. Kendle

This is a work of non-fiction.

All rights reserved. No part of this book may be reproduced or transmitted in any form or by any means, electronic storage, and retrieval system, except in the case of brief quotations embodied in critical articles or reviews, without permission in writing from the publisher.

In no way is it legal to reproduce, duplicate, or transmit any part of this document in either electronic means or in printed format. Recording of this publication is strictly prohibited and any storage of this document is not allowed unless with written permission from the publisher. All rights reserved.

All scripture reference from the New International Version of the Bible unless otherwise stated.

ISBN: 978-1-943409-97-6

Published by Pure Thoughts Publishing, LLC

2055 Gees Mill Rd #316 | Conyers, GA 30013 USA

470-440-0875 | www.purethoughtspublishing.com

Printed in the United States of America

DEDICATION

To my son DeMarion D. Morgan - My life transformed the day you were born and you are the greatest blessing to my life. I dedicate this book to you because the Lord has made sure you never wanted for anything. I am forever grateful for every moment we have encountered on our journey. Everything I have gone through is for you and favor is all over your life. From this moment forward, everything you put your hands to will prosper and succeed.

I dedicate this book to Rilee S. Thompson, one of my favorite nieces whose presence has helped me get through many things. We have a bond unbreakable.

I dedicate this book to my grandmothers Chandria Howard and Jewel Kendle (2015) as well as my great-grandmother Gloria Woodard "Mama Woods" (2020). All three of you have been a blessing, adding value to my life and teaching me so many things.

I dedicate this to my parents Dion Woodard, Sr. and Michele Kendle for bringing me into this life to be who God has created me to be.

I dedicate this book to those who believed in me and stood by me through the ups and downs. You have all played a vital role in my life at some point. When I made mistakes and wanted to quit, you were right there to pull me up. Thank you Denita Vidrine, Issac Williams, Kalima Woody, Kerry Nicholas, Lionel Negrete, Ronnique Garner, and Tinisha Jackson. Thank you, Delilah Battle, for always helping me with DeMarion and taking him in as your own with no hesitation. A special thank you to Shenna Bradley. Your inspiration gave me the boost I needed to release this book. I am truly grateful for you all and pray nothing but blessings and prosperity over your life.

I dedicate this to my STL (Earth City) pastors David and Nicole Crank for being responsible for increasing my faith to another level. You have inspired and helped me more than you know. My degree of faith has increased to allow me to walk in authority and believe on another level. I am grateful for the day I walked into your church; my life has never been the same. I thank you for being open to allow the Lord to use you to deliver the word to me and so many others, and for staying true to his word in the last days no matter what people said or thought about you. I pray that God keeps on using the both of you.

TABLE OF CONTENTS

INTRODUCTION 1

CHAPTER 1 4

A Gain Over a Loss 4

CHAPTER 2 10

Forsaken But Not Held Back 10

CHAPTER 3 19

The Fight of My Life 19

CHAPTER 4 25

Girl, Get Up 25

CHAPTER 5 37

Radical Transformation 37

CHAPTER 6 52

From STL to Houston 52

CHAPTER 7 70

From Fear to Faith	70
CONCLUSION	100
ABOUT THE AUTHOR	106

INTRODUCTION

Have you ever wondered why certain things happened in your life? Do you ever feel like one thing after another keeps happening? Let me be the first to say that I asked myself Why? so many times I wore myself out. When we are going through challenges we have so many questions we want answered about "why" that we tend to bring unwanted stress to our lives. Stress then leads to anxiety and anxiety leads to fear.

A more modernized description of fear is "false evidence appearing real". It is when something that is not true comes across as real. For example, we know there is not a real Freddie Krueger but when we watch a horror movie, characters like him appear real. No matter how old the movie is or how many times you have seen it, you still are fearful watching it because the scary character seems real.

The same thing happens when we face challenges that lead us to ask "why?" If you think about it long enough, you will begin to believe those thoughts are reality. In all honesty, do we really want to know the answer? If the Lord gave us all the details of his plans for us upfront, would we have really wanted to go through the things we went through? I am almost certain you would say no.

I wrote this book not because of the why but because of the who. I am hoping that my testimony and some of the things I experienced will help you to understand the who behind the why. This book is not only just for single parents but for everyone who has encountered adversity along the way and feel like everything you're going through is in vain. I am here to tell you that nothing you have been through has been wasted and there is a purpose and plan designed for your life that you can only accomplish if you finish the race. The race is never given to the fastest or the strongest; rather, it is given to the one who can stick it out until the end. You don't have to be perfect, you just have to be willing to fight through the urge to quit or give up.

I pray that everyone reading this book is inspired and encouraged to go after everything you put your mind to. Don't worry about the why or even the how, but focus on the who. I am telling you the darkest parts of my life to tell you not to quit. There were many times I wanted to give up but it was God's strength and favor in my life that kept me going. Revelations reminds us that "They triumphed over him by the blood of the Lamb and by the word of their testimony" (BibleGateway.com, Revelations, 12:11).

I don't claim to have it all together because everyday is a challenge. But it's what you make of the challenge that helps you make it through challenging times. I did not write this for accolades; I wrote this book to tell you there is purpose behind your pain. If I can get through it as a single mother then you can do anything, and it all starts with you. We can't always change the circumstance, but if we change our view of it, then the circumstance will eventually change for us.

CHAPTER 1

A GAIN OVER A LOSS

It was October 24, 2006 at 6:00 am. You should have seen the excitement on my face. After dropping out of college, running to the ER for false labor, and nine months of carrying a heavy load, my due date was finally here. I had my bag packed the night before, and I walked into DePaul Hospital fully prepared to deliver. When I arrived, Dr. Fisher prepped me to induce my labor. My water broke but the contractions did not come right away like I assumed they would from what I witnessed on TV. The doctor advised it could take 12-24 hours for the contractions to start coming after the water breaks. They didn't really begin to kick in until later in the day. When the contractions became unbearable they decided to give me an epidural. I was not really paying attention to the time because the epidural gave me so much relief, I didn't realize we were already half way through the next day.

The nurses and doctor frequently came in to check on me to see if I had dilated more, but I still hadn't dilated enough. The last time they came in to check on me they realized that my baby was stuck to my pelvis. Three days after being induced, I hadn't dilated enough and the doctor insisted on performing an emergency C-section to deliver the baby. On October 27, 2006, at seven pounds, nine ounces and 21 inches long, DeMarion Morgan was born. I was on top of the world because I gave birth to a cute, cuddly little boy. Holding my son in my arms for the first time was like a dream come true. I always wanted a boy and a girl. But I wanted the boy first so he could protect his little sister. I didn't realize that God had great plans for this child and his birth date would have meaning behind it. I gained a king's kid, a child of the most high king. I experienced a range of emotions because I didn't deliver him the day I was induced, I had to have a C-Section that I was not prepared for, and deal with my son's father's inconsistent presence in our relationship. However, what look like inconveniences are really a part of God's plan for our life. After all the misery and pain I never knew I was giving birth to the next world changer and that the number 27 would have an impact on the generations to come.

The bible tells us in Isaiah "For my thoughts are not your thoughts, neither are your ways my ways, declares the Lord" (Isaiah, 55:8) What I saw as an inconvenience turned out to be a blessing. I had to remember that God does everything in perfect timing. I never planned to have a child right after high school but when my son graced this earth, my entire life changed. On the 27th of October, I officially became a mother and had no idea what was to come.

I had been a mother for about 6 weeks. I was in the house everyday, all day, with this new baby, not really getting any time for myself. I was limited in what I could do because of the C-Section. I felt unreasonably stressed.

Well, another reason I was under a lot of added stress because I had gotten pregnant again and my son was not even two months old! I was an emotional wreck, with thoughts running through my mind such as I don't want to go through this again and I can't raise these kids by myself. I was already going through enough stress being at home with one baby and not enough me-time. I decided I wasn't going to put myself through the additional stress so I had an abortion. I wasn't ready to raise another child by myself.

Many people assume having an abortion is easy and quick and you move on with your life. It is nowhere near that simple! The emotional pain after losing a child from an abortion is much greater than the pain experienced from having a child and not being able to care for it. The guilt from that decision ate at me and I fell into a deep depression. I was devastated and felt I murdered my child. I kept having flashbacks of how my baby looked when they pulled it out of me after the procedure. I grieved over the loss of my child, thinking everyday I just killed the little girl I always wanted. I wrestled with guilt and grieved over my loss for several months because, deep down, I never really wanted to get rid of my baby.

It wasn't until a few years ago I began to realize that the mistakes we make do not stop God from accomplishing his plan and purpose for our lives. The Lord sees all and knows all; he is Alpha and Omega, the beginning and the end. He knew my mistakes before I even had the chance to make them. In Jeremiah, we are reminded that "Before I formed you in the womb I knew you, before you were born I set you apart: I appointed you as a prophet to the nations" (Jeremiah, 1:5). The things we do and choices we make never catch God by surprise. No matter how many times we mess up, he still loves us. No matter how many times we claim we are not going to do something again, he is still right there. His grace covers us because there is no mistake we can make through which his grace will not sustain us. He is just that good. If you look back over your life, you will notice that every adversity was preparing you for the next level.

What I considered to be a loss was not a true loss. Instead, it was a gain. I gained a wonderful son I am able to pour myself into, and give the undivided attention he needed to succeed in life. My son had a major impact on how I began to live my life and changed my life for the better.

Things don't always happen according to how we plan for it to happen. We have these preconceived ideas of how old we want to be when we get married, how old we want to be when we have children, the age we will buy our first home, and so forth. One thing about God is that everything happens according to His timing. He knows exactly when we are mature enough to receive what we are asking for. Even if we make plans to have a baby by a certain age or get married by a certain age and it does not happen at that specified time we must still believe. A delay is never a denial; it just means it is not time yet. What appears as years to us appears is seconds to God.

The mistake I made in one season of my life does not stop God from fulfilling His plan for me in another season. I can still have the daughter I always wanted, I just have to continue to believe that his ways are not my ways and His thoughts are not my thoughts. The Lord has a way of making the impossible look possible creating a blessing in the most inopportune moment, when we believe.

CHAPTER 2

FORSAKEN BUT NOT HELD BACK

In the beginning part of 2008, I thought I was living my best life. I was partying with my friends every other weekend, meeting new people, and just having fun. All of a sudden, things began to change. My mother hit me with the news that she was moving to Atlanta, GA, in a few months. DeMarion was two years old at the time and my mother had kept him for me since the day he was born. She kept everyone's children, including mine when I went to work, went out partying, and when I just needed a break. The news put me at a crossroads because I really did not trust anyone with my child and, truth be told, I relied on her as my permanent babysitter. She talked about moving to Atlanta for several years, but I didn't think she would move so soon. All I could think was How could she just leave me? What was I going to do? I was no longer going to be able to run to my mom's house anymore, and that is when reality started to sink in.

When my mother finally left to start her new journey, the challenges of motherhood really kicked in. I enrolled my son in a daycare in one of the worst neighborhoods, but at the time as a single parent, it was all I could afford. I would get off of work fearful that someone would rob me when I picked up DeMarion because at the time people were walking up on women in the neighborhood and snatching their purses. However, no matter the circumstance, I didn't give up. A year later, when my lease was up, I decided to move into a better neighborhood so he could go to a better school. I wasn't making much money at the time but somehow God made a way for me to get a nice apartment in Cottleville (St. Charles, MO) under affordable lease terms. The apartment was huge, the area was nice, and I found DeMarion a daycare that was right down the street. The daycare had cameras I could log in to and see what he was doing, and the teachers were really nice. All of this was like a dream come true. Yet the downside was that after I paid all my bills, I was only left with $1 to my name. This was an amazing opportunity but it was a huge sacrifice. How in the world was I going to make it off $1 until the next time I got paid?

I was literally living check-to-check, and my child support payments were inconsistent. Sometimes I would go more than six months without receiving anything help from DeMarion's father. There were so many nights I would just break down and cry, and, if I am being honest, during that time I didn't have a solid relationship with God the way I do now. I knew of God and attended church but didn't pray until there was a need and didn't seek God the way I do now.

We all know what happens when there is no relationship with God — we take matters into our own hands. We were blessed to receive food stamps at the time so we didn't have to worry about food. I did whatever was necessary to provide for my child, but didn't take the consequences into consideration.. Many people didn't know this at the time, but when DeMarion's would outgrow his shoes or need clothes, I would walk right into the store and put the shoes or clothes in my purse and walk out.

I didn't like asking for help. All too often, people would tell me they would help but would not follow through. I was still stuck trying to figure it out. I wasn't proud of the choices I made but that was my life without God. I am so grateful that even in my wrong choices God's hand was still upon my life and he still showed me favor.

I eventually ended up having to pull my son out of daycare just to keep gas money in my pocket. I was paying $180 a week for daycare on top of a car note, rent, and other bills that my paycheck could barely cover. I found Head Start, and it was $35 per week, but DeMarion couldn't start until he was three years old. He only had 2 months left before he turned three so one of my relatives told me I could pull him out of daycare and they would keep him for me for $40 a week until he started Head Start. I was so excited because I was finally going to catch a financial break, but things never turn out how they seem. I ended up pulling DeMarion out of daycare and she kept him for a few weeks only to come and tell me she was going back to school and I had to find someone else to watch him. I was extremely upset because I made arrangements, trying to get my life back on track only to be thrown right back in the same situation. Even after being forsaken by a relative I still did not quit. Somehow God worked it out again and I found another person to keep him for the last month. There were still challenges with this other person, but God saw fit to put them in position until the very end to fulfill that need.

After experiencing all of that you would have thought that I would be able to catch a breath and things would start to look up.

The following year all hell broke loose. I lost my job, my apartment, and my car all in a matter of months. The blessing out of all of that was that I still qualified to receive unemployment, so I had some income after losing my apartment. I asked to live with both my parents, my siblings, and other relatives and they all turned me down. I shed so many tears because I was really going through a rough patch and no one wanted to help.

The only person to open the door for my son and I with no restrictions was my grandmother, Chandria. My grandmother was staying with her ex-husband at the time but she refused to leave us out on the streets. We slept on an air mattress in her ex-husband's basement and everything appeared to be going well. One day he got so upset about me washing clothes late at night and decided to kick us out, including my grandmother.

At this point we were back to square one with all my stuff in storage and nowhere to go. I took a leap of faith and forced my way down to my mother's house in Atlanta, GA. I asked her before if we could stay with her, and she told me that we were not welcomed. I took it upon myself to go anyway. I still had my car, so I packed all of our clothes and headed to Atlanta. I figured she wouldn't turn down her child and grandchild when they were on her doorstep, and she didn't.

I was given another chance to start over and get my life together. It was not home, but I did my best to make it feel like home. Regrettably, I was only there for 2 weeks and my car got repossessed. How they found me over 500 miles away in Atlanta but not in St. Louis I'll never know. I still have no idea to this day but it seemed like I was in a never-ending battle because I didn't have a car, I couldn't find a job, and I couldn't get DeMarion in an affordable school. At this point I felt like giving up because I had no clue what to do next. Then one day, my friend Gabe reached out to me and said, "My door is always open for you all if you need to come back home." Those words were music to my ears because it was easier to maneuver in a more familiar place. She was indeed sent by God because she only wanted me to give her $20 a month to help with toiletries. I was so grateful I ended up giving her $100 a month instead.

My plan was to be at Gabe's house for only two or three months, enough time to get a job and move into my own apartment. It is funny how we make plans but they never turn out how we expect them to. My two- to three-month contingency plan ended up being an extended stay for 10 months longer than I had expected. It seemed like things went from bad to worse, and I started to wonder if I made the right choice coming back. Even though DeMarion was back in school and I finally saved up enough money to get a new car, I still kept going through bad things. When I got the new car it was broken into a few weeks later. DeMarion's dad came to stay at Gabe's house as well for a few months because his brother lived there. I went through so much during those few months he stayed there. We got into several physical fights daily over his lies, cheating, and playing with my emotions. I felt so hurt and alone. There was not a day that passed by I did not shed a tear resenting my situation.

All the things I went through in my first couple months of moving back to Missouri made me feel as if I was not going to make it. Shortly after the first few months of chaos, I finally landed a job interview. I got up early to get dressed and take DeMarion to school and got pulled over on our way there. The police officer claimed he pulled me over to make certain that my temporary tag was valid. When he ran my name, he learned that my license was suspended for not paying a ticket in another state. I showed him the receipt from the money order I bought to cover the fees for the ticket, but he did not believe me. The officer arrested me and called a wrecker to tow my car.

DeMarion immediately started crying when he saw they were putting us in separate police cars. I still remember the look on his face as he turned around patting on the window of the car, crying out saying, "No mommy no, I want my mama." With tears rolling down my face I kept pleading for the officer to understand that this had to be a mistake. The officer kept ignoring me and saying he could lock me up for a long time. When we made it to the police station I made a phone call to my dad to get me out because I knew I paid the ticket. The officer softened up a bit and told my dad to use the money he was going to bond me out with to get my car out the impound yard. Even though the officer was being reasonable with my dad, he still was cruel to me. He handed my son the key to take the handcuffs off me and released us to sit on the curb while I waited for my dad to arrive. This had to be one of the most unethical experiences I ever had. DeMarion was so shaken up by the experience that when I went to drop him off at school that day he cried thinking I was going back to jail. Those 10 months felt like the longest 10 months of my life. I felt like God had forsaken me and left me to suffer.

At the time, I didn't realize that God's hand was on my life, even in the darkest hour. He was always right there. It is difficult to see the light at the end of the tunnel when you are going through the dark. We must realize that there is always pain before the promise, and every breakdown is a setup for a breakthrough.

A few months later, a temp agency called to offer me a temp-to-hire position. I was so excited that I did not waste any time. I took my second paycheck to go find an apartment for DeMarion and me. I was kind of nervous because most apartments would like for you to be on the job for at least six months or check stubs to reflect you can pay the rent. However, God seems to show up at the right time because I got approved for a duplex with only two check stubs from the temp agency. God is so good that even when we don't deserve it or we choose to go our own way he is right there to pick us up. Deuteronomy reminds us to "Be strong and courageous. Do not be afraid or terrified because of them for the Lord your God goes with you, he will never leave you nor forsake you." (Deuteronomy, 31:6) When people forsake you, God is still with you. No matter who you are and what you have done, He still loves you and is right there waiting for you. Many people seem to walk away from God but He never walks away from us. People change, your circumstances will change, but God's word will never change. It takes courage and faith to trust in Him when your world seems to be falling apart. It may not have felt like he was with me in those moments, but when I look back now, I see that God never forgot about me and He most certainly will never forget about you.

CHAPTER 3

THE FIGHT OF MY LIFE

It was the early part of September 2011 when I moved into my duplex, and it felt like a breath of fresh air. It felt like I had my own little mini-home because it came with a driveway and basement that included a washer and dryer, and it just felt like home. I made a vow to myself when I moved in that DeMarion and I would never be homeless again. DeMarion was finally old enough to go to regular school. The exciting thing about it was DeMarion attended one of my childhood elementary schools and some of my old teachers were still there. The school offered after-school care that allowed me enough time to get off work and swing by to pick him up. I re-enrolled in school and even got back into church. Things were finally starting to look up for us. Life was starting to appear normal again, at least for a little while. Do you know when you feel as though something is too good to be true? That's what this was - too good to be true.

I was grateful to be in my own place again, but this move led to a series of events that really taught me to lean on God. I felt inclined to believe every year I was fighting for my life, my sanity, and my peace. I lost my job more times than I can count, I constantly fought with my son's father for cheating and then would take him back, and other events occurred. Anyonewho knew me then knew I always relied on a job to sustain me. I believed that if I did not work it was the end of the world. I would never miss a day at work unless absolutely necessary, because as a single parent with no help, I couldn't afford to miss any money. I remember DeMarion got sick on the 4th of July and at most companies, in order to get paid for the holiday, you have to work the day before and the day after. He was so sick that I had to take him to the emergency room, where the doctors diagnosed him with whooping cough. They prescribed him a steroid and he needed to stay home for at least 24 hours after taking the medicine. I panicked because I needed to go to work the next day to get paid for the holiday and the day before. My supervisor was a real stickler and usually did not budge for any last minute time off requests. But God was already at work; when I reached out to my supervisor, she told me I just needed to bring a doctor's note and I would still get paid for all my days.

I was grateful to still have my job, but I was always looking for opportunities to increase my income. A few months later I took a position with another company that paid very well with bonuses every month. I loved this job because I had one of the greatest supervisors. He was so cool that sometimes I had to pinch myself to see if I was being pranked because I came from more strict work environments. He believed in a work-life balance, and I did not have a difficult time taking time off when I needed to. It was like a blessing in disguise and everything I hoped for in a job. About after a little less than a year they came in to tell us they were laying us off. The layoff was sudden and unexpected, but we received a severance package that included three months of pay and benefits.

In the beginning, it wasn't bad because I was still getting paid and I could stay home. However, when time started running down and I couldn't find a job, I started to panic. I didn't know what to do next. This was when I was really able to build on my relationship with God and learn to trust who He really is. God was teaching me that my source is not in a job, it's in Him. The job is just the tool. At the time, I didn't recognize that each time I lost my job, God brought me through, and he would get me through this, too. He is the same God who was with me when I lost everything and the same God that was still with me in this loss as well. Something kicked in and I realized that prayer was the weapon I needed for this fight in this season of my life.

While I was building on my prayer life and Christian walk, I was tested many times. Some of those times I was tested, the way I responded you would have thought that I wasn't a Christian at all.

DeMarion's father had an affair with one of my childhood friends that started when he was 6 months old. I took him back each time because I didn't want my son to grow up without a father in his life. He went back and forth between us for years, until one day I got fed up. We got into an argument earlier that morning that ended in a huge fight. After being laid off for a bit I finally started a new position but our son got sick, and I asked him to pick DeMarion up from school. He refused because he was mad about the argument we had earlier that morning. I knew he was trying to pick a fight on purpose to go back to the other woman. I rushed home from work throwing him and his belongings out of my house then we started physically fighting. He pushed me to the ground, slamming me so hard I bruised my rib cage. I was hurt badly enough that I couldn't laugh or move.

After about 15 minutes of fighting the police were called to break us up; he got his things and left.

I replayed that scene over and over in my head finally making a vow to myself to never go back. I was tired of fighting to prove my worth to people. One thing my godmother Valencia would say, and it never resonated until that moment, is "Teach people how to treat you Brit." Pastor Keion says, "Anyone that does not appreciate your presence should earn your absence." After going through years of unnecessary heartache and drama I did not realize that God saw me when others didn't

God always gives warning before destruction. There were several times God would intervene on my behalf but I kept forcing my way back into situations that were already over. One thing we must remember is the Lord gives us free will and even when our will is out of alignment with Him, He will never force His will upon us. If that were not true then it would be easy for everyone to be saved. Many would say well if God loved me then why would He let me go through difficult times. We need to ask ourselves if God ever told us to get involved in those situations in the first place. When he gives us free will that means we have a choice and that choice determines the path we take. The path can either lead us to destiny or lead us to misery. However, even if you take the path to misery, the moment you call on Him and give up your life to serve Him, He can turn your misery into ministry. What the enemy meant for evil He can always turn it around for your good.

CHAPTER 4

GIRL, GET UP

Even after leaving years of a toxic relationship, I was still in a vulnerable state of mind and couldn't fathom being alone. I continued to stand firm on my decision of never going back to DeMarion's father because deep down I knew I deserved better. After being single for a few months, I decided to go out with my best friend Alicia to attend her cousin's birthday gathering at Dave & Busters. It was always fun hanging out with her family because I had a crush on her cousin and I knew he had a crush on me, too. This particular day, while I was sneaking a look at the cousin, someone else was sneaking a look at me. A handsome server stopped me on my way to the bathroom, told me he was interested in getting to know me, and asked for my number. I gave him the side-eye at first, like What can you do for me? You work at Dave and Busters. He continued to pursue me and told me it was his part time job and he really wanted to take me out. So, since he was cute, I gave him a shot.

We talked on the phone for hours, as if we were in high school. Kevin was a real gentleman and very sweet. I was really impressed with his care and concern, but he still didn't know where I lived, even after two months. I understood why he felt the way he did, but I was very protective of allowing people in my living space because I did not want anyone around DeMarion. When I finally let my guard down and started to feel comfortable around him, I didn't realize I had opened the door to the date from hell. It was the biggest mistake I made and all that sweetness was mixed with a mental illness of bipolar schizophrenia.

There were days Kevin stayed over, and every morning I would watch Bishop TD Jakes' sermons. He would wake up some mornings and out of nowhere and say, "B***** turn that s*** down. I gotta go to work." I would get angry and kick him out, but as soon as he called to apologize, I took him right back. It had gotten so bad that he would buy groceries for me, then take all the groceries out of my house after an argument. I couldn't believe that I went from one dysfunctional relationship to another.

I became so immune that many times I didn't even recognize myself. Kevin was horrible and his kids were even worse. One day, DeMarion had one of his teammates over and Kevin's kids came over too. We ran to the store, his children jumped DeMarion's teammate while we were gone. I was so furious with him that I made him take his children and leave. There was a time we were sitting at the kitchen table and he told me out of nowhere his ex girlfriend put a spell on him. I called my sister and asked her to start praying for him and as she was praying, he laughed an evil laugh that shook me so deeply I sent him home. There were so many warning signs, I don't know how I ignored them.

The relationship went from bad to worse in a little over four months. One day my son was in Ohio with his coaches playing in a basketball tournament. Kevin felt it was the perfect time for a romantic night at my house. He came over, cooked, and we watched movies. He stayed the night and everything went well. The next morning he got up to use the bathroom before he started to get ready for work. When he came out, I started joking with him saying" You are not gonna wash your hands with your lil nasty self." He instantly got upset and started calling me out my name so I started going off on him. Before I knew it, he walked into the room and smacked me so hard I fell back and stumbled to the ground. This was the first time he had ever hit me, so I was shocked and angry at the same time. I tried to run to the bathroom to grab my phone but he ran behind me and snatched it out of my hand. At that moment I feared for my life so I started screaming as loud as I could in the bathroom. The walls were very thin and I wanted my neighbor to hear me. When I started screaming he immediately ran out of the bathroom, threw my phone, and ran out the house. The moment I knew he was gone I quickly ran out my house and banged on the neighbor's door. I asked her if I could use her phone because I needed to find my phone. I kept calling my phone and finally found it behind the couch. The first person I thought to call was my brother because I had just spoken with him earlier that morning. I didn't realize he was at my dad's house when I called because shortly after we hung up he was pulling up to my house with my dad and uncle in the car. They hopped out of their car, asked where he lived, and went looking for him.

Eventually they found him walking up Jennings Station Road and they pulled over on a gas station lot. Everyone hopped out of the car. My dad tried to be the peacemaker; my brother and uncle did not want to do any talking because they were ready to tear him up. My dad asked Kevin if he hit me and he said no. My uncle yelled out, "Then why was she holding her face when we pulled up?" Kevin said he didn't know. My dad told him to never contact me again, and I would never contact him. Nevertheless, this is how deranged Kevin was. As my dad was telling him this, he was dialing my number to prove a point — that he would call me whenever he wanted. They eventually ended up leaving, but not before giving me a lecture about leaving him alone, and that I deserved better. In all honesty they were completely right and I was so grateful they came to my rescue because things could have turned out much worse. As I stated before, the Lord will always provide a way of escape;, it's just up to us to take advantage of the opportunity. Many times we put ourselves in these situations because we don't wait for God's best in our lives. We are in such a hurry not to be alone that we don't realize God's best takes time and does not happen overnight. Instead of taking time to heal from years of one broken relationship, I jumped right into another, taking myself down another road of unnecessary detours.

After the incident, Kevin continued to call me even after I told him not to. He kept calling daily to apologize until one day I finally gave in and we started talking again. I didn't tell anyone we were communicating because I didn't want to look stupid, so I kept it a secret.

One particular night, he wanted to take me out to dinner at a Mexican restaurant I loved called El Maguey. The waiter got us a table three seats away from the door. He sat with his back facing the door and I sat where I could see who came in the door. I just so happen to look up and who walks in? My dad and his girlfriend. I was so nervous, like a little kid in trouble. I bent my head down so that he would not see me. Well, that did not work because he ended up walking towards our table to get to his table and we made eye contact. My dad looked over at my ex and gave me the most deadly stare and said, "Hey Brit," and I said nervously, "Hey dad." Kevin tried to reach his hand out and give him a handshake but my dad turned and walked away. I was every bit embarrassed, nervous, and scared all at the same time. I knew that it was hard for my dad to see me with yet another guy that was not good for me. To be honest it was hard for me too; I had no clue what I was doing with him, I just knew I did not want to be alone.

About a month later I ended up getting a call that my grandmother Jewel was rushed to the hospital and she may not make it. My grandmother had just been in the hospital a week before and had seemed to be doing well, so they released her. A day or two after her release she passed out and was rushed right back to the hospital. My emotions were all over the place because I was very close with my grandmothers and would do anything for them. My grandmother Jewel and I were really close. I took her to the store, we talked on the phone, she practically called me for everything and I would do my best to make whatever she needed happen. My grandma Jewel became very fond of Kevin because anytime I needed to see her or do something for her he was with me. She loved him because he would make her laugh and just get her whatever she needed. When I got the call to come up and say our goodbyes because she was not going to make it, he went up to the hospital with me. We stayed for a few hours, then more of my family started to come up so we stepped outside to let them go in and get the chance to say their goodbyes. After a while he got impatient and started yelling at me to take him back to his car because he had to work in the morning. I gave him a look as if, you can't be serious right now. He did not have to be at work until 1:00 pm the next day. He continued to yell and started to be a bit disrespectful, so we hopped in my car and I took him back to his car.

When the funeral came, Kevin couldn't make it, so I went to his job afterwards because I just wanted to be comforted. When I came to see him, I gave him an obituary but I couldn't stop crying, and he said to me," You can't be coming up to my job doing all that crying, you have to leave doing all that." I felt so humiliated and unappreciated that I just walked out and did not say a word.

What woman wants to hear their man tell them to stop crying over a loved one they just lost? In that moment I knew I had stretched this relationship way beyond the time frame it should have been and I was starting to mentally check out. I felt as if I needed to do something to get my life back on track and find myself again.

I spent many years juggling school part time and working full-time. I finally found a school that had an accelerated program that would allow me to gain more credit hours to graduate sooner. The only requirement was that I had to attend school one night a week from 6pm until 10pm. The average person would have thought that wasn't too bad, but it was. I couldn't find a steady babysitter to keep DeMarion. Every person that agreed to keep him would eventually renege on me, leaving me in a terrible position with no other options. I got tired of people saying they would help but never keep their promise. So I taught DeMarion how to stay at home by himself at the age of 8 years old. I purchased him a minute-phone to stay in contact. I would rush home from work to pick him up from school, grab him some food, make him take a shower, and then head right back out. There were many times I was late for class because I had to make sure he was together before I went back out. I would call him on every break and on my way home. As a single parent, you do what you have to do to make it work, but there were many times I wanted to quit because it was so hard leaving my child. But I kept pushing.

The death of my grandmother Jewel, attending school, being a single parent, and having a psychopath for a boyfriend was all starting to take a toll on my mental health. There were many nights I couldn't stop crying because it was just so much to deal with. I felt like I was losing myself, so I started stepping out and trying to find me. I already taught DeMarion how to stay at home by himself so he had gotten used to it. I hung out with one of my brother Stephen because I hadn't been out in a while, and had the best time. We went out so much that I became a regular at this bar I loved and knew everyone. When I hung out it gave me life and I felt like I was on top of the world and no one could tell me anything. I thought I was living my best life drinking so much and not remembering what happened or how I got home. Wasting money every weekend on alcohol, smoking, parties, clothes, and so many other things assuming it would make me happy.

This one particular night it was my birthday; my cousin Sheree and I always celebrated our birthdays together because they are only a few days apart. We went to a bar we regularly went to, but also stopped in another bar and met some guys. They were buying us drinks all night and we smoked hookah and we were having a good time. When the bar closed we did not want to go home, and one guy invited us to his house which was across the street from the bar. Let me remind you that in my right mind I would have never taken him up on his offer: however, alcohol will make you do the strangest things. We headed to this random guy house and hung out drinking and smoking hookah. For some reason, I was more sober than my cousin because I noticed she was starting to pass out. I was not going to let her pass out at this guy's house, so it was time for us to go. I called my Kevin to help get both of our cars back to my house. I drove her truck and he followed me in my car. Somehow he took a detour and didn't follow me completely so I got nervous because my Sheree was passed out in the back and I told him to get my car to my house. When he finally made it, I hopped right back in the car to drop him off at home. He started being disrespectful, calling me out my name. I didn't argue I just kept saying "yeah, ok" and "this is why I'm done with you." I pulled up to his house to let him out and he took the cup full of liquor in my console and splashed it all over me, then ran. I had just gotten my hair done and liquor was all in my hair, clothes, and everywhere. I screamed the word, "B****" so loud that even the neighbors heard me. I pulled in front of his house and started throwing things at the windows because I couldn't find him. I pulled off to head back to my house and he called me 15 minutes later saying his grandmother was sick. I didn't care about him or his grandmother at the time and told him not to ever call my phone again. This was the day I decided to never deal with him again.

I was tired, stressed out and drained from his disrespect, jealousy and anger. I could not take another day of it. I felt completely tapped out and refused to take another hit. He stalked me for about a year after the breakup but I already made up in my mind I was never going back. Many have heard the song by R-Kelly, "When a Woman's Fed Up". The song is so true because women will take and take and take so much from a man until they finally explode, then they're referred to as "crazy". We give them chance after chance not realizing when enough is enough. I fell into this category many times. I put up with months and years of dysfunction because I wasn't confident enough in myself to know I deserve better. What kind of example was I setting for DeMarion on how to treat women? I took these men back several times before I realized I could do better. Isn't that a lot like how we do Christ? We go to the other side many times before we realize we need him. Putting ourselves in unnecessary situations, begging for his forgiveness and he still takes us right back. When you know who you are and who is for you then nothing can hold you down. Philippians reminds us that "I can do all things through Christ who strengthens me" (Philippians, 4:13). There is a coach that will stand in the fight with you till the end and his name is Jesus. My coach stood on the sideline saying,"Girl, Get Up, I will take it from here." Insecurities, fear, and rejection will keep you in a cycle of pain, which is not God's will for your life. His plans are for you to prosper and succeed. Failed relationships or past mistakes should never stop you from reaching your purpose. Mistakes happen but it is the part we take from the mistake and learn from that makes us who we are.

CHAPTER 5

RADICAL TRANSFORMATION

After 10 years of attempting college, I finally made it to graduation the year of 2016. I made a promise to my grandmother, Jewel Kendle, that I would stick it out in school until the end, in hopes that she would be present for the victorious moment of me walking across the stage. Although she couldn't be present, the day of graduation I knew she was smiling down, proud that I had finally finished my Bachelors Degree in Health Management. All I could think was that it took me 10 years to finish, but I finally made it. After years of struggling, I was grateful to finally get a chance to make a better life for me and my son. If you were anything like me, you'd assume after graduation, the career doors start bursting open and you make all this money. Unfortunately, at the time I wasn't educated on the process enough it does not work that way. Most jobs want you to have experience in your field before they decide to hire you, even if you have the degree. They do not care about the money you spent on college and years you spent trying to attain your degree. I was discouraged because I had worked in banking most of my life, so trying to get someone to take a chance on me in healthcare would be challenging. I applied for several jobs and was not really getting any responses. It wasn't until I lost my job at the bank that doors started to open for me.

However, when I first lost my job, I was devastated. I had just come back from vacation for my birthday and they let me go out of nowhere. This was the third time I lost my job in the last six years and I began to think What is wrong with me? What was I gonna do? I wasn't getting child support consistently and I did not have anyone to rely on. How was I going to maintain my car note, bills, and provide for my child? Everytime I took a step forward, I felt like I was kicked several steps back. However, the loss of my job taught me to seek God and trust his timing. I began to draw near to Him and He began to show me that He was in control and could take care of me without a job. I developed a routine where I got up every morning and walked around the lake, staying physically and biblically fit. Some of my audible moments with God came from walking around that lake. I learned so much in that season of my life that I probably never would have learned had I had a job. My relationship with God began to grow more and during this phase of joblessness. The more I sought God, the more doors I saw open for me.

After about a month, I finally landed a job at a health center as the assistant manager. This was a blessing in disguise and a huge jump for me considering I had never been in healthcare before. I was so excited about landing the position that I didn't realize there would be challenges that I definitely was not ready for. Every day someone was calling off, leaving the manager and me to cover those areas. The job already required us to stay late one night a week, and if someone didn't make their shift we had to cover the remaining time. Everything was just a mess and there was always drama. Employees could not get along and I was left to deal with the issues when I had several issues of my own. The job was so stressful that I would wait in my car three minutes prior to clocking in before I would go in. When I took time off, I never wanted to go back; I complained, and would look for reasons not to return. Well, it was not long before God gave me exactly what I was asking for. About a month later, right after coming off another vacation, I lost my job again. For a moment I thought I was cursed because everytime I went on vacation I came back jobless. The issue with this job was they were investigating an incident between two employees and to this day, I do not understand what I had to do with that incident.

Nevertheless, in all honesty, I was not upset at all. I never felt so much peace in knowing that God had my child and me covered. The peace of God that came over me before starting this position carried me after I was let go, reminding me to keep trusting God through it all. The circumstance did not define who I was and did not change who God is. Shifts in our lives will always occur in uncomfortable places.

My fourth time without a job required me to take another route and try something different. We can't keep doing the same thing expecting a different result, so this time, I went on a fast. I actually fasted twice—once for seven days and the other for three days. When I say the Lord really spoke to me during the fast and took me through the beginning stages of healing. I journaled all my experiences and some of the things he spoke to me are currently manifesting. One of the things he said was that my life was going to take off really fast and that it would shock the people around me and provoke them into change. I was excited but I had no idea what that looked like and wanted everything to happen right then. I did not realize God always prepares the place before he performs. He would always whisper, "Do not be afraid, stand still and see the salvation of the Lord" (Exodus, 14:13). Little did I know that he was already preparing the place for me to transition but I just could not see it yet. "Now faith is the substance of things hoped for and the evidence of things not seen" (Hebrews, 11:1). What seemed like years to me was a matter of seconds to God. Even when I couldn't see that he was doing, he was definitely at work. We all tend to grow weary because of our circumstances and we do everything to try and get ourselves out of our current circumstances to minimize the pain. In those moments we do not realize that the pain is a part of the promise.

Both fasts accelerated my desire to lean into God's word more because so much was occuring in my life. I lost a few people along the way that I thought would be with me till the end, my unemployment payments were getting ready to run out, and I still hadn't found a job. However, God continued to show His faithfulness because a temp agency contacted me about a three month assignment. It was not much but I jumped on it. On my last day of the three-day fast, I had worked in this position for about two weeks when another agency called me back for a temp-to-permanent position with an organization I had been trying to get hired with for months. I was excited because this was the moment I had been waiting for. After hearing the details, though, I became discouraged. The position would not pay the money I expected and it was for a position at the very bottom of the organization, scanning documents. My attitude wasn't that great at the time because I was confident I had come too far in my career to go back to the bottom. Nonetheless, during this three-day fast, the Lord reminded me of the things He told me, which was to hold on and be patient. Despite how things looked, it was all going to work out for my good. Accepting the new position was a humbling experience but it also opened up greater opportunities. At that time I did not realize that God was ordering my steps and I was stepping in affirmations that are currently manifesting.

I decided to accept the offer and leave my current position with the other temp agency two weeks later. The day I was supposed to start, there were some issues because they were still waiting on the background check to come back and my start date was pushed back for another two to three weeks. The recruiter advised this had never happened to them before, but I was more upset because she brought this up at the last minute. I had just left a job that brought in a steady weekly income to again being without a job or income. I tried to call the other temp agency back but they had already found someone to fill my position. I called the recruiter and told her what happened and that she was going to have to find me something asap to fill in that delay. She told me they only had it in their budget to fit me in for one day. I broke down crying, wondering why this was happening to me, and my sister, Tinisha, kept saying, "Brit you know where your help comes from so stop worrying." I was so grateful for her because that is exactly what I needed to remind me how far I had come. I got a call a week later from the recruiter about a position at a school scanning books for a week. The pay was very low and the drive was forty minutes from my home. I was so unhappy and felt like my life was spiraling downward. I contemplated whether or not to take it until Tinisha stepped in again, reminding me that God had me. I remember hanging up the phone with her and hearing the Lord speak to me clearly asking why I was worrying about my source of income when He has taken care of me thus far. He said that if He could take care of the birds and the trees, then He is well able to care for me also. After having an encounter with the Lord, I accepted the position.

During this time there was a speaker named Jonathan Shuttlesworth coming to our church for a week of revival July 23,

2017- July 28, 2017 at 12noon and 7:00pm. I had never heard this man preach or speak a day in my life, but the church kept playing his videos in the announcements and his voice would never leave my conscious saying, "Your life will never be the same." Those words played over and over in my head and I was determined not to miss out.

My new position didn't start until the last day of the revival, so I attended every service he had and I am so glad I did. The revival was one of the greatest experiences of my life. I was getting filled and fed by the Holy Spirit so much that I was bummed about not being able to attend the 12 noon session on the last day. Surprisingly the position did not work out and I was able to leave early and attend both services. Even though the position did not work out, I had peace in knowing the Lord was with me.

I have not mentioned that my mother walked away from believing in God shortly after my grandmother passed away. I don't know what happened, but I know that it was heartbreaking to hear she no longer believed. I remember my Tinisha and I were talking to Jonathan Shuttlesworth at one of the 12 noon services. We told him we were worried about our mother. He turned to us and said, "Don't worry, your mother will be saved before I leave." The last night of the revival, the spirit was flowing so heavily that my mother was saved. I screamed at the top of my lungs because it was a joy to see God show up and transform her. He laid hands on all three of us and I remember him saying to me, "The power of God is all over you and everything you have been praying for is coming to pass. And the next six months would be the greatest six months of my life."

I had already started declaring over my life it would be the greatest six months, but my definition of greater and God's definition of greater were totally different. The Lord has a funny way of positioning us to receive a miracle or blessing. He will put the right people in place at the right time to get His will accomplished. When the Lord told me my life would take off quickly, I was thinking right in those six months, never realizing until now that it was the foundation to get me where I am today. I wasn't really expecting to get any bad reports since it was the greatest six months of my life but the saying "It always gets worse before it gets better" was a qualified statement for that time. When I finally started the new position, I was lucky enough to get another cool manager. After working hard in the temp role for a few months, taking on extra duties, and staying late, I felt it was only fair to discuss next steps. He was working on a plan to hire me full-time permanently, but he ended up accepting another position which delayed me in getting a permanent position. Shortly after, I landed an interview for a permanent position in that department, only to be turned down a week later. I wasn't receiving any benefits and could not take off or I would not be paid. I couldn't afford to pay his basketball expenses or really get him anything for Christmas. It was a blessing the coach worked with me on the payment and for Christmas I went to Family Dollar and wrapped up some gifts. Even though my career was not moving as fast as I had hoped, the position kept teaching me to trust in the Lord.

Things were not looking so good on the career side and the Lord had already revealed to me my time was up in my current apartment. I had been there for seven years and was not interested in leaving because I was comfortable there and afraid of being homeless again. We all know that when the Lord says move and you don't move, circumstances arise that force you to make a move. I never had any issues with anyone in all the years I lived there, but began to get into it with my neighbor over silly things that led to large disputes. This went on for months and it physically and mentally drained me. I wondered how was I going to move on from a temp job. I thought about seven years prior how God made a way with the same circumstance, so I stepped out on faith and started looking.

It was a struggle, but when the new year approached things started to radically transform. In March of the following year, I attended Faith Church St. Louis because one of my favorite speakers, Toure Roberts, was going to be there. I had been listening to Toure and Sarah Jakes everyday while working and did not want to miss the opportunity to see him live. I also wanted to check out the church because I heard so much about it - good and bad - and just wanted to judge for myself.

The day I went, I fell in love with the church and the people. They always made me feel welcomed and they never pressured me to give. It was like a breath of fresh air, coming from a background of churches where the collection plate was passed 20 times and you were guilted into giving. Some of the previous churches would also make you feel horrible for the mistakes you made and gossip all about you. Faith Church wasn't like that. They made you feel loved, valued, and you were never alone. It was never about the money for them but more on increasing your faith, and boy didn't they impress me! I was so pleased with the service, worship, and fellowship that I ended up joining a few weeks later. Pastors David and Nicole Crank taught me what it was like to have real, unshakeable faith in God.

The moment after I joined the church, it seemed like things in my life began to progress and get better and better. The church taught me how to tithe properly and when you tithe correct you get double the blessing. Things were beginning to shift in my current role and I connected with another supervisor who helped me land a permanent position in the department she was transitioning to. It was going so well that a couple months later, I found a townhome in a nice school district that put me 10 minutes away from my job and provided my son quality education. I was nervous about moving because my rent would increase by $350 and I did not know if I could afford the rent based upon my current income. However, God was working even when I didn't see it. We must remember this "For where two or three gather in my name, there I am with them" (Matthew, 18:20). The Lord blessed me with a friend named Tiffany who prayed with me and stood in agreement with me that God would meet every need. Nonetheless, the Lord never ceases to amaze me because he opened the door for me to live comfortably in the townhome that I wanted and it put me closer to my church. I started serving in several ministries. DeMarion connected with other teens in the church and built up his relationship with the Lord. Blessings were flowing, God was opening doors, and my life was not the same.

The vision for the church—people connect, families grow and lives are changed—was really happening in my life. I was starting to see my life radically transform before my eyes. I built new friendships, a church family and connections with others that helped accelerate other areas in my life.

Even though I was grateful we were in a better place, it was still difficult because raising a child alone requires so much work. My child was no longer a baby but transforming into a young man. DeMarion has played basketball since he was four years old and running him back and forth to practices, games, and traveling with his team, all while trying to create a better life for us was difficult was no help. The more he grew up the more he needed physically, mentally, and spiritually. I did not feel capable of giving him everything he needed. How was I going to begin to understand the things a boy needs when I am a woman? Needless to say it seems like everytime I was in fear the Lord would send someone or show me that He could meet every need. The scripture from Psalms says, "Though my mother and father forsake me the Lord will receive me" (Psalms, 27:10). This scripture has been in DeMarion's room since he was seven years old. Although his earthly father wasn't present like he should have been, his Heavenly Father has made sure DeMarion has never lacked in any area. The Lord sent coaches, mentors, and uncles into my son's life to provide whatever he needed. A few people counted him out, sold him false promises and did not believe in him. But those that did stick around made a significant impact. I developed a support system with other parents on the team who would help out with the picking up and dropping off to practice or games. Our life had begun to radically transform for the better.

Challenges occur in everyone's life beyond our control. Single parents tend to get hit with the most challenges because we are doing it by ourselves. Parenting does not come with a manual and we can't control what happens to us. We can control how we navigate through the challenges and be the best parent we know how to be. The weight that you carry will be different from another person's weight because God has called us all to do something different. More weights are applied when you are walking into a new level and for those that can handle the new level. There is a saying, "new level, new devil". Anytime you go up a new level there is always a new devil or pressure waiting for you. However, pressure makes diamonds, and if you want to be a diamond, you have to be willing to be cut. Many people want the blessing but don't want to go through what it takes to get the blessing. When the Lord says it's time for transformation no one and nothing can stop it. He put the right people in place at the right time to get his will accomplished in my life. He hid me for the perfect time and season to promote me. Always remember this, "The Lord never takes his eyes off the righteous. He honors them and promotes them" (Job, 36:7). Keep your eye on the end goal and not on the circumstances because God has a way of suddenly changing your circumstances.

CHAPTER 6

FROM STL TO HOUSTON

When I look back at every experience I had, I would have never imagined it would be the setup for where I am today. I wasn't happy in my current role, and hadn't been since the day I started. But I accepted it in hopes that within six months I would get promoted or transferred to another role.

I worked hard those six months to get transferred to another position, then suddenly the guidelines changed. Internal employees had to wait a year before transferring out of a department. If you were getting promoted within the department,you only had to wait six months but if you were transferring out of the department you had to wait a year. I applied for so many positions within the department since I had made it to my six month mark and got turned down for each one. I was more than qualified for every position I applied for, but the leadership always came up with a reason as to why I did not meet the criteria. I came in with a plan and it intimidated them. They tried everything in their power to ensure I did not make it to the next level.

My supervisor at the time was about my age and not too concerned with being a leader. Her goal was more focused on impressing the leaders above her. There are too many people in leadership roles who have no idea what it takes to lead a team. There are leaders and then there are dictators, and there is a huge difference between them. A leader sets their employees up for success, whereas a dictator just gives orders, not really expecting anything less than what could benefit them long term.

In this case, my supervisor was a dictator and no matter how many times I would discuss with her my goals for my career within the department, she never took any initiative to ensure I was any closer to achieving those goals. I was one of the hardest working employees in the department, working 24 hours a week in overtime. Let's just say I was the true definition of a team player. I took every initiative to ensure the department succeeded while they took every opportunity they could to make me suffer.

The department did some restructuring and I was put under another supervisor who watched me like a hawk. He was the worst male supervisor I had ever had. If I went to the restroom too long he was looking for me; I was literally being harassed by him on a regular basis.

"And we know that God causes all things to work together for good to those who love God, to those who are called according to his purpose" (Romans, 8:28). When you are chosen by God he causes all things to work out in your favor. When you are his child he will move people out the way to get his will accomplished on the earth. The enemy's tactics are never greater than God's anointing. Needless to say, the supervisor was let go before the new year and I was put back under the original supervisor that I had. I was a bit relieved but was not thrilled because working under her again put me back in the same situation.

The new year was approaching and I was tired of being harassed and not progressing. I was overworked, underpaid, and undervalued. The department developed a training initiative that would bring more work in-house. The training initiative would help the department grow and save the organization money. It was a great opportunity and I thought it could have a positive impact on my career. I inquired about it several times with leadership. They kept giving me the run around and not telling me the truth. I was told by one person in leadership that the people were selected from a drawing, and another leader stated management selected. However, when I found out that an employee, who had only been with the company for three months, was selected over me, I was furious. I was so tired of being overlooked and passed over that at this point I just wanted out. I would cry and pray on my way to work everyday, asking the Lord why I was there and why I felt like I wasn't progressing. He reminded me of one of my favorite scriptures, "Let us not become weary in doing good, for at the proper time, we will reap a harvest if we don't give up" (Galatians, 6:9). This scripture gave me so much life that I memorized it and quoted it everyday on my way to work.

Going into the next year, I knew my time was up in St. Louis because nothing seemed to be working in my favor. I felt suffocated and stuck, with no ability to grow or progress. I started thinking about moving out of state.

Let me give a brief overview on why Texas was my first option. I had always talked about moving to Dallas, TX, to become a member at Bishop TD Jakes church, The Potter's House. I watched him every morning and listened to just about every one of his sermons, so I had an idea of where I would end up. Two years prior, I had taken my son and one of his friends to a Dallas Mavericks basketball game and we had a great time. My son and his friend were able to go on the court and shoot with Kyle Lowery and DeMar Derozan before the game started. They both even got their shirts autographed as well. About halfway through the game a few seats were empty in front of us so one of the hosts was nice enough to move us closer. I felt so much peace in the city of Dallas that I knew it was somewhere I wanted to be. However, through my dedication to watching Bishop TD Jakes sermons faithfully, another pastor caught my attention.

I never heard of this man before, but this particular Sunday, he was phenomenal. He was a guest speaker at Bishop TD Jakes church and his name was Pastor Keion Henderson. He preached a sermon called, "The Danger of an Oil Leak". This pastor was so real, authentic, and relatable that I found myself watching his sermons and Bishop Jakes every day. The impact and change that he had on my life influenced my family, friends, and coworkers as well.

It was about a year later when my sister and I went to visit his church in Houston, TX, for my birthday. We had such a good time from the moment we got there until the time we left. Service was awesome and hospitality was great so we extended our stay for a few hours to attend the 1:30 pm service at the downtown location.

After the service, one of his assistants, who, by the way, was very hospitable at each service, asked if we wanted to meet Pastor K. I was grateful because I wasn't expecting to see him at all and most well known pastors usually don't have time to stop and say anything. I have never been one to make a big deal over meeting someone well-known because I consider them to be just as normal as anyone else. However, when Pastor Keion came out, he totally changed my perspective. He was very engaging and he sang Happy Birthday to me! How cool is that? I started thinking this pastor was definitely the real deal. It was one of the greatest experiences I had ever had.

Pastor Keion reminded me of my current pastor at the time, Pastor David Crank. One of the reasons I was afraid to leave St. Louis was because I really loved my church, Faith Church St. Louis; we were a family. I was so involved, I loved the people, and the people loved me. I never complained about serving, I loved the environment, and I loved my pastors. I was at church faithfully every Sunday. I was impressed that Pastor Keion expressed a selfless act of not being so high up he couldn't come down and interact with others. I did want to leave my current church until I found one led by the same type of pastor as Pastor David. In that moment of meeting him, I knew that nothing could stop me and it was safe to say I found my pastor, so I could make my move. Having such a great experience in both cities left me torn between moving to Dallas or moving to Houston. I mean, who could pass up the opportunity to be under the great Bishop Jakes, someone I admired since I was a teenager? Not to mention I felt peace in Dallas. The more I began to seek God, the more I realized my move was bigger than that.

It was finally a new year and I knew it was time for change, so I knew a fast was needed. Normally I went on a fast in January every year anyway, but this time it was different. I did not want to make any moves without God involved, nor did I want to put my son through any drastic changes if it was not in line with God's will for our lives. The year before, when I was ready to leave, the Lord told me it was not time yet, and I needed to make sure this time was the right time. I went on a seven-day fast for completion and to confirm my next move. I even created a vision board because Pastor Nicole kept preaching about vision. Pastor Nicole showed us her vision board at church, which motivated me to make one. On this vision board, I had Dallas on one side and Houston on the other. Most of the time when you fast you don't get the answer right away. God does things in his own time and knows the appointed time when to provide a response. If I could be honest, I did not get an answer from the lord until after I bought tickets to a Houston Rockets game. I arranged to take a trip to Dallas the following month to look at some apartments there. However, it seemed like everytime I tried to plan a trip to Dallas there would be some conflict and it would not work out. When I began scheduling appointments to look at apartments in Houston, the Lord said I would then receive my confirmation after my trip.

We arrived in Houston on a Friday and spent a day and half looking at apartments in the Woodlands and Cypress area. The Rockets versus Timberwolves game was not until Sunday so we had plenty of time to explore and do other things. Both areas were nice but after driving around I realized the Woodlands was too far from everything. The more I looked in Cypress the more convinced I became, and they were rated as one of the top school districts for athletes.

When we went to visit our last apartment for the day in Cypress, my son was exhausted and tired of looking at places. He told me he would sit in the car until I was finished. The one I went to see was very nice but the leasing agent advised they did not have any with garages available. She told me that people don't really move out of those. I was advised to check back closer to my move and see if anything was available.

After visiting the apartments, I took my son to an AAU basketball tournament to get a feel of the teams and who he might want to play for. We attended a championship game and met with the coach at the end. The coach and I exchanged numbers and I told her I would be in touch once we made the move. My son had been through a lot playing on some of the best teams, but always being overlooked and not valued. I believed the move to Texas would give him the opportunity to really showcase his talent and not be limited. We both were excited after leaving the AAU game.

That Sunday, we attended the Lighthouse Church and the NBA game that evening. We had great seats sitting eight rows back from the court. Overall we had a great time and just like the Lord had said, after that experience I knew where I was moving to. When I got back home I created another vision board, but this time it had Cypress, TX, on one side with the apartments and The Woodlands, TX, on the other. In the middle of the vision board it said, "Move to Houston with an amazing job in healthcare by July 12, 2019."

My experience in Houston helped me change my perspective about my current position. I started working as if I was working for God and waiting on him to make a move. I started to apply for jobs in Texas and got a few interviews but somehow was not getting hired. The jobs either wanted me to start right away or to already be living in Houston. I continued to pray daily and lean on God for the doors I needed opened. There were definitely times I worried but the lord kept proving his faithfulness.

Our department had a meeting and we were advised that leadership was restructuring the department again because they replaced the previous supervisor. If I could be honest, I was not too enthusiastic about this meeting because this would have made my third supervisor and I already did not trust any of them. I begged my supervisor at the time to keep me on her team. I was familiar with how she operated and knew that there changes always were sketchy. She laughed as if she did not know how it was going to work out, only to put me right under the new supervisor. Genesis tells us, "You intended to harm me, but God intended it for good to accomplish what is now being done, the saving of many lives" (Genesis, 50:20). This scripture spoke directly to my situation because my new supervisor Carrie turned out to be an angel sent from God. Who would have ever thought

God put her in position to get His will accomplished for my life? I spent so many months fighting to get to another position and no matter how hard I worked I kept getting looked over. However, God is in control of all things and when He says it's time, then that means it's time. They did not know that God was hiding me for such a time as this to accomplish His will on the earth through me. When you are faithful God will move you from the back of the line to the front of the line when it's your time.

I had to stay in constant prayer during this time because I was dealing with so much in those first few months of the new year. My son was getting into unnecessary fights at school and his grades were slipping. It was evident I needed to leave St. Louis but I wasn't sure how. I did not have the money and I was not having any luck landing a job. Nonetheless, I kept pushing and was determined not to get discouraged. I continued to repeat Galatians 6:9 everyday until it resonated in my spirit.

Carrie was like a breath of fresh air and one of the greatest supervisors I ever had. She listened and saw so much potential in me that she was committed to ensuring I made it to the next level. Every time an opportunity would come up in the department she would try to submit me for it but it would get pushed back. I was determined not to quit, so I got my resume revised and started submitting applications outside of the organization. I ended up getting a callback from a healthcare company; the manager and I talked for a while. He was so impressed he set me up for a second interview with two of his colleagues. Little did I know that the company that revised my resume added a few key skills to my resume I was not aware of, and those skills were brought up in the interview. It caught me off guard when one of the managers questioned me about them. I had no idea how to respond and basically blew the whole interview. I was really bummed because I was counting on this job as my ticket out, and I was running out of time. I was due to either re-sign my lease or put in my 60-day notice within the next two weeks at my current residence. I didn't want to move without a job so I kept praying, and I'm talking about around-the-clock praying. I prayed on my way to work, at 10:30 am, on my lunch break, and at night because the Bible tells us to pray without ceasing. I needed a miracle and I needed one fast, and the only one who could answer that prayer was my Heavenly Father.

For some reason on this particular day, I kept staring at my vision board because it was embedded in me that the more you see something the more you believe it. The Lord kept telling me to put in my notice but I was hesitant. I went on a fast for about six hours, prayed, and finally put in my 60-day notice at my apartment on the last day. I want to point out there is power behind fasting and if you are ever in doubt go on a fast. Shortly after, something in me said to call the last apartment we visited when we were in Houston. I was confused because this apartment was not on my vision board. I did not include it because the leasing consultant told me the one I wanted would not be available.

Nonetheless, I decided to give them a call anyway. When the leasing manager picked up, I asked her if they had any two bedrooms with a garage and she told me they did and it would be available on July 12, 2019. I was in shock because if you recall earlier in the chapter I discussed that I created a vision board stating I would be moving to Dallas or Houston by July 12, 2019. I went on to ask her what all I needed to apply as that was the time I was trying to move and she told me I could apply with my current pay stubs. I was overwhelmed with joy because I was stressing the whole time about needing a job to get a place. But then I was hit with a dilemma, the application fee was $50 and I did not have the money until the following week. I told her I would call back to apply next week when I had the money and we hung up the phone. The manager called me back fifteen minutes later and said, "Ma'am I do not want you to lose this place, so go ahead and fill out the application and you can pay your application fee when you get paid." I hung up the phone crying and thanking God because he literally showed up right when I needed him to. He has a way of making things happen we never saw coming. I couldn't help but to keep giving him praise. What looks like an obstacle to us is simple to God. No matter what it is, he will come through if you believe. It is even better when you witness his goodness for yourself. Most apartments need an offer letter or some form of documentation confirming your employment, they even want their application fee upfront. With ongoing confirmations this was a move setup from God, it gave me the courage to fight harder.

My application was submitted and a week later I was approved, but I still did not have a job. When you are expecting something from the lord, counterfeit opportunities always show up to distract you from achieving what he has promised you. All of a sudden, one of the managers in another department reached out to me about a position that I inquired about nine months prior. I was excited but I kept thinking, I reached out several times about this position and I never got a response so why now? Several thoughts ran through my head about why I should take it and stay in St. Louis. I really wanted this position but I knew it was not from God. I decided to pray about it and the more I prayed the more I believed it was not a move from God but a trick of the enemy to keep me stagnant. I knew I had to be patient and keep believing.

A week later, I received an email that I was being considered for a job internally I forgot I had applied for. I was never considering a job internally since I was turned down for everything I applied for. I was excited when I saw the email come through, so I filled in my friend Michelle and my current Carrie with what was happening. Carrie and I had a long talk because before she gave recommendation to the hiring manager she wanted to be sure this was what I really wanted.

Shortly after our conversation I received a call from the recruiter to schedule an interview. I remember it like it was yesterday, my interview was on May 30, 2019. I studied and prepared for that interview all night. The number 30 represents the blood of Jesus and I believed the blood of Jesus was covering this position for me. The interview went well and we were on the phone for two hours. The hiring manager did advise that they could not offer relocation expenses if I were chosen for the position. I told her I was ok with it because I was already prepared to move either way. I remember writing my offer letter in faith and praying over it, believing I got the job. The next day the recruiter reached out to me looking to extend an offer. The Lord had already given me a salary amount to ask for and it was the same amount in the offer letter. I presented it to the recruiter and she advised she would send it over to the hiring manager and get back to me. It felt like the longest wait ever. I started praying the Lord would send me a 24-hour financial miracle. A few hours later, I received a callback from the recruiter advising that my salary request was accepted and they also were offering an additional $2,000 in relocation expenses to move. Prayer changes things, all you have to do is believe. God does some of his best work in dark places so that we know it was him. Keep trusting God for everything and doubt Him for nothing. Your faith is the key to help you win on the next level.

Landing a job was one of the biggest challenges during this transition. I had to keep believing in the vision even when I did not see it happening as quickly as I wanted it to. Everyday, up until the move I faced distractions that were eager to make me lose focus. I was worried about my son and how his school year ended. It was like the enemy planned to attack all my relationships because I was in conflict with everyone, including my parents. I was worried about my mom having a place to stay before I left and my dad was just being evil. I kept arguing with my sister over things I don't even remember. Nowhere was safe and I had no one to call on. There was a moment where I panicked and actually wanted to give up on the entire move to Houston. In that moment, the Lord reminded me to be like a tree planted trusting in God and not focusing on what was happening around me. My faith had increased another level, but it required me to be bold to step out of the familiar and walk into the unfamiliar. Faith is risk-taking, and I could not allow the fear of failure hold me back by playing it safe.

The day had finally come to say goodbye to St. Louis and hello to Houston - July 12, 2019. My house was packed up and we were ready to go. July 12th signified my life in comparison to Abraham, the Lord told him to leave everything that was familiar and go to an unfamiliar place (Genesis, 12). I gave up everything I knew to accept what God was trying to do for me. I would always wonder why I didn't fit in with certain friends or family members. It wasn't until that day that I realized I was called to be set apart. From the day I was born, the Lord chose me to break the cycle in my family and stand out. He put me on assignment not just for me but everyone connected to me. Remaining comfortable eliminates growth and hinders success. Elevation will always be inconvenient but if we never take the risk we will never receive the reward.

CHAPTER 7
FROM FEAR TO FAITH

We finally got the chance to settle in and I began to reflect on all I went through to get to the present moment. There were so many things that went wrong along the way that made me want to give up. However, I remember my best friend Kerry telling me labor could be painful but the delivery is sweet. I was giving birth to a vision that the Lord wanted to release. Anytime you give birth, it can be painful but there is always a promise waiting after the pain. In order to experience the abundance of what the Lord has for us, we must let go of any expectations or limitations on how things should be and deliver what He has placed on the inside of us. He is a God with no limits and can make things happen at the right time. God won't let us know how or when it will happen, He just makes it happen so that he gets the glory.

I had a week before I started my new position, so I began to study and consecrate myself in the Lord. I did not understand my purpose for being in Houston and wanted clarification for the purpose behind the move. I started studying the book of Genesis and the Lord stopped me in chapter six where He speaks about His disappointment in the world being out of control. The Lord reminded me that in the last days it would be like the days of Noah and wickedness would be treated as normal. He showed me how the city of Houston was prosperous but full of wickedness and darkness that appears as normal to those who live there. In the times of Noah, the Lord responded with a flood to get the attention of the people. Houston had already been hit with floods from Hurricane Harvey in 2017, two years prior to me relocating. The Lord spoke to me and told me I would be used as a vessel to turn the hearts of unbelievers and believers and assist my new pastor with leading people in the city back to repentance. When the Lord revealed this, I kept thinking, Are you sure Lord? How in the world is this going to happen when this man does not know me? I had to realize that I can't worry about how, I just have to trust in who was going to do it. . The Lord's ways are greater than our ways and if He said it then it shall come to pass.

As true believers, we can't keep letting people we love miss out on the opportunity to receive salvation. We have to take a stand for what is right at some point in order to see real change. The bible tells us, "You can identify them by their fruit, that is, by the way they act. Can you pick grapes from thorn bushes, or figs from thistles?"(Matthew, 7:16). Will you take a stand for Christ even if you have to stand by yourself? When people see God's faithfulness in your life it sparks their curiosity or provokes change. We have to come together to diversify the way others view Christ or the church. If you continue to read in Genesis, he told Noah to build an ark out of cypresswood and everything in it would be protected. The Lord orchestrated a plan for my son and me to move to the Cypress area, so that during our transition we would be protected from anything that comes our way. It was that God would provide me with such deep revelation and orchestrate everything in my life to fit HIs promise.

Although I clung to His promise, if I am being truthful, I still had doubt. I remember crying myself to sleep for the first few weeks because I was in a new city, a new place, and I did not know anyone. I felt so alone making such a drastic change to our life and it was settling in that there was no turning back. I was away from both of my grandmothers, away from my church, my family, my friends, my exes, and pretty much everything I knew. All I had was the Lord and my son. I thought about packing up and going home many times. I was such a people-person that I despised the idea of being alone. I knew how to be alone, but this was a different level of alone that left me no choice but to depend solely upon the Lord. Not depend on my loved ones, coworkers, or friends, but only on God. I began to think maybe it was set up this way to build on my relationship with my son and build my relationship with the Lord.

Eventually I began to change my mindset and start looking at my situation differently. I started to become grateful for how far I have come, which in turn built my character and gave me strength. The more I built my strength the more issues started to occur. I started having issues I was not expecting with my manager. However, I could not let those issues distract me from the reason I was in Houston. Changing how I saw the situation allowed me to get through those issues. I had become close with a coworker whose husband was battling cancer. She wanted to move to Houston so that her husband could receive better treatment. I called up some of my close friends that could bombard heaven and get a prayer through. We were all in agreement that things were going to transform in her life. She came to me the very next day and said she was not sad anymore because she knew God had a plan for both her and her husband. It was the best thing I had heard since relocating to Houston. I was grateful to see the Lord lead me to someone to help them believe.

It was time for me to get back into the swing of things, so I decided to visit my new church. My sister and I went to visit the year prior and we had a great time. However when I returned to visit as a resident, I was surprised to find that the experience was not so not the same. It was the total opposite of what I had experienced the first time. The people were not welcoming or friendly; if you sat in the wrong section, you were asked to move. I kept thinking this is not what I was expecting. The difference in the environment threw me off because it was not what I was used to. I asked the Lord, Are you sure you sent me to this church? I stuck it out for as long as I could but eventually ended up leaving the church for about a few weeks and started visiting other churches.

I wanted to find a church that fit my personality, where the environment was welcoming and it was not a hassle to serve. However, when you make moves that are not in alignment with God's purpose, the Holy Spirit will convict you. The lord never told me to leave. I took it upon myself to leave. I remember sitting in the other church service and the Lord spoke to me clearly, asking me how I would see His promises fulfilled if I was out of position? How would I know if he is the God of the impossible if I wasn't in a situation that looked impossible to change? When God is silent, it does not mean he is not working behind the scenes. We just have to trust that He will turn things around in our favor. We must stand in the good times, bad times, and pressure-filled times to make it to the next level. The opposition we encounter always has purpose behind it. The decision to go back was not easy because I felt so disconnected from the environment but I knew the reason I moved to Houston was bigger than me. I had to focus on the promise and not the people, trusting that God would work on the people's heart. What we believe in troubled times determines how we come out of it. After going back, I still encountered a few challenges, but this particular Sunday gave me a sense of peace about returning. The pastor decided not to follow regular protocol and opened the opportunity for those that wanted to serve to do so. I was relieved because God knew exactly what door needed to be opened to gain that connection again. Sometimes the Lord will call you to be a light that shines in dark places. Although it may be dark in that moment the light will eventually eliminate what was once dark.

Fear will make you see things in a negative perspective. The enemy will try to steal the peace from where you are to keep you from where you're going. Although things were working out in the spiritual part of my life, I was still unhappy with the personal part of my life. I was tired of being alone and did not want to just attend church and go home. I wanted to date and connect with others, but it was so hard. Even though I told myself I would never do this, a few of my friends suggested dating apps. This time I figured why not, it's a new city and could be a great way to get to know people. I connected with a guy and we hit it off well. I really liked him because he seemed to be the perfect gentleman. It was like a dream come true because my son loved him, my grandma loved him, and pretty much everyone around me loved him. He would do anything for me and my son, I started thinking that Houston was not looking so bad, after all. However as we continued to date, I noticed some things just did not add up. He couldn't answer the phone after a certain time, I was never able to go to his home, and a bunch of other weird things happened that did not make sense. After putting all the clues together I found out he was living a lie and living with another woman. All I could think about was why can't I seem to get this relationship thing right? It was one of the most painful experiences I had encountered because it was the first breakup I had to deal with alone. No family to run to, friends couch to cry on, or no additional guy to fill in the gap to help me get over him. Breakups are tough but necessary. It zaps your energy and takes your focus off what God is really trying to do through you.

Relationships are like a cracker jack box —you never know what you get until you open it. We must watch out for those relationships that will prey on your heart and rob you of your purpose. I refer to these relationships as violators of the heart because they tell you what you want to hear and take advantage of the love you want to give. This seemed to be exactly what that relationship was. Even though the enemy may have intended for it to take me out, God used it to protect me moving forward. We get into these relationships because of the choices we make but, even when we make bad choices, the Lord always provides a way of escape. Cycles can only be broken when we identify and accept when a relationship is not working. He loves us so much that He creates the red flags early on to prevent us from a lifetime of pain. Doors close as a sign that there is something greater in store on the other side.

People come into your life for a season, a reason, or a lifetime. Whenever they come we must learn to embrace them while they are there and let them go when it's time to move on.

One of my coworkers saw what I was going through and refused to let me go through it alone. We became very close, hanging out often and meeting new people. She adopted my son as her godson and we had such an amazing time that I no longer worried about the breakup.

There were only two months left in the year when my friend decided she wanted to go to church with me. I was excited because many times, I tried to get her to come to church with me but she was not able to because of her schedule. Pastor Joel Tudman spoke that Sunday and I remember we both left crying, transformed with better perspectives. After church a couple she knew began to prophesy into both of our lives. They referenced for me to claim Psalms 91 & Psalms 121 over my life. God was going to give me deep revelation and I would become a student of the word by studying Greek and Hebrew. I would have an influence on faith and have increasing faith for the path God had me on. I would be a kingdom financer and have multiple streams of income. I would be so wealthy that I was going to attract other wealthy people to help cover more in the kingdom. Everything was getting ready to upgrade in my life - what I drive, where I live, and the way I see myself. I was told that I would be getting married soon and be a pastor's wife, and it would not be a long courtship. A baby was coming shortly after the wedding. DeMarion was going to be successful with basketball and he was going to receive scholarships. They told me to be sure DeMarion does not connect with any Deliliah's and pray he connects with his soulmate.

If you've ever been to any form of revival and the speaker prophesied, it feels like they never really prophesy to you when you want them to. When those pastors spoke into my life, I was excited but shocked because a part of me was not sure how credible the information was. I was more shocked because I preferred to date a newly saved man, I never thought twice about a pastor. My jaw dropped when I heard that. However, a part of me felt there was some truth behind what they were saying because the other things discussed were starting to happen. It also gave me the confirmation I needed to determine if I was headed in the right direction. When I ended the year, I created another vision board and list positioning me toward the goals I hoped to achieve. I got my son involved in creating a vision board as well so he could see there is power behind our words. Habakkuk states, "And the LORD answered me: 'Write the vision; make it plain on tablets, so he may run who reads it. For still the vision awaits its appointed time; it hastens to the end—it will not lie. If it seems slow, wait for it; it will surely come; it will not delay' " (Habakkuk, 2:2-3). Whatever it may be that you are expecting God to do in your life, write it down, set the wheels in motion to accomplish that goal and watch it come to pass. Whatever you sow into your vision or dream, you will get back double if you remain committed to it.

When the year 2000 (or year 2K) came, I remember on December 31, 1999 everyone thought the world was about to end. The news and other media outlets had everyone so scared that they did not want to go to sleep. Well, 2020 was sort of similar to the year 2000; the only difference was that instead of being told the world was going to end, in return the world shut down. I remember declaring on December 31, 2019 that 2020 would be my year and I know this might seem like a shocker to most but it really was my year. It was not only my year, but one of the greatest years for my son as well. It started out a bit rough with many obstacles that tried to stand in my way, but I overcame them, finishing out strong. Obstacles and adversity never catch God by surprise. He will move what looks like an obstacle or mountain out the way to accomplish His will in your life.

Walking into 2020 was rough because even though I did everything right I still hit bumps in the road just 30 days in. I started the year correctly fasting and praying like I normally do, but alignment with God's will did not exempt me from being attacked. The enemy is always alert and on the prowl, setting up traps to see who he can destroy. Heading into the second month of the year I got into a car accident and lost my new friend, all in the same month. A few days after the accident, she decided she wanted to end the friendship. I felt it was coming because she had been acting strange for weeks. It did bother me at first because it happened so suddenly, but I had to realize everyone that comes into my life is not meant to stay. When you are headed toward greatness, everyone that rode with you can't go with you because they may not be beneficial to your long-term success. I quickly switched my focus to trust that God knows best and to not allow the end of something to distract me from the beginning of something greater.

When the car accident occurred, I had just picked DeMarion up from school and on my way to the office to drop off a report. I was at a traffic light when a truck ran into the back of my car and left the scene. I pulled over to look at the damage; it was not as bad as I feared. There was a pretty big dent in the back of my vehicle. Even in the midst of a crisis, God was still showing me favor because when I got out of the car to check my car, I found the other party's license plate on the ground. I picked it up and called 911 to report the accident. The pain from the accident did not kick in for us until shortly after, requiring a trip to the emergency room for both DeMarion and me. I was still in pain, and needed physical therapy to recover.

The process of trying to fight to prove my innocence was one of the most difficult things I had to experience. The police gave me a hard time trying to file the report. One of the officers blamed me for the incident because the other driver went back to the scene after I left to file a report. The police department was having a hard time locating the initial 911 call I made. This process was extremely stressful and I wanted to hire an attorney.

The first attorney I hired could not do anything for me and I had to do all the research. They spent a few months playing around with my case, leading me nowhere but to tell me they could not help me. However my second attorney was like an angel sent from heaven because he appeared out of nowhere and got right on my case. I still don't remember how I found him or he found me, but that is how you know he was truly sent from the Lord. When the challenges you face are in alignment with God's plan he will put the right people and resources in place to help you fight your battle.

The pandemic started in March of 2020, the same week my son was scheduled to play in Alabama. I remember we were excited about going to Alabama because we had never been, but the tournament ended up being cancelled. My son and I were determined to not let the cancellation stand in our way so we changed our plans and drove to Atlanta instead to see my niece, Rilee, and my mom. We had a good time, then as soon as we came back, the shutdowns had begun.

The next day, when I went back to work, I was sent to work from home until further notice. I looked at it as a blessing in disguise because we were already working from home a few days a week. My son was on spring break at the time and they continued to push their return date back until they decided the students would not return. In the beginning it was fine because I needed that time to rest but after while I was over it. Since I was already at home with my son, I had my sister Ashley send my niece Rilee down to spend a few weeks with us. They initially told us that we would work from home until the end of April but when they kept pushing the date back, I told my Ashley that Rilee could stay a little longer. She eventually ended up staying with us for the entire summer. Believe it or not, Rilee and DeMarion helped me grow in more ways than I could have ever imagined. Rilee reminded us of our nightly prayer together. We had a lot of ups and downs but I built a bond with those two children that is irreplaceable. We had many good days where we went to water parks, arcades, parks, dinner, and so many other things. However, there were also challenges. It was frustrating being a full-time teacher, cook, mother, trainer, and every duty you can think of. Regardless of the challenges, the benefits still outweighed the challenges and I would give anything to treasure those moments I had with them..

Early in the pandemic, I was riding home from a site visit, listening to a sermon from Sarah Jakes Roberts. When I created my vision board a few months earlier,I included a picture of Sarah Jakes preaching, but with my face. I had a note with it stating that I should be speaking to people around the world about the goodness of Jesus and serving Him at a young age. While I was listening to this sermon, I kept saying, Lord this is gonna me someday, I can't wait til the day you use me. The Lord spoke to me clearly and said, "I am using you now. I want you to go home, study, and record yourself speaking, then release it. I pondered on it for days because I was not sure what I was going to talk about and if people would even bother to watch.

When I finally did buckle down and do as God asked, I did not know what to do or how to do it; I only knew I had a phone that would record a video and I did it. I recorded it in my bed titled, " The Peace of God in the Midst of a Storm" and uploaded it to YouTube. It actually turned out better than I thought it would. My video received 156 views, and a lot of people thanked me for sharing it. They said that they were looking forward to the next one. I just wanted people to see that someone just as regular as them can achieve anything if you keep our focus on the Lord.

Eventually I began to study more and pray more, recording videos every other week. I got better using different angles, different backgrounds, and I became more fluent with my words. It became a win for me because I was digging deeper in the word and the Lord was still getting the glory from it. It also helped me deliver better presentations at work. There were many times I wanted to quit because of the opinions of others or if I touched on a topic that many did not want to hear. However, I had to remember that only the things I do for Christ will last and, it did not matter what they think but what He thinks. I continued to make the videos because it was what the Lord wanted me to do and they got better and better.

The COVID-19 pandemic impacted not just one group of people or one nation, but the entire world. We went from living a life we thought was a normal life to where what was considered normal has changed. The new normal for 2020 is not leaving your home without a mask on. We often take the small things in our lives for granted, assuming the ordinary will always be there. We did not value or appreciate the freedom we had until it was stripped away from us. The Lord has a funny way of getting our attention when he wants to get his will accomplished on the earth. Just like the days of Noah, where He responded with a flood because he was displeased with the way people were acting. Well He responded in this season with a pandemic, which was designed to slow us down, refocus our attention on Him. The Lord needed to see who would take a stand and really trust his word or who would put their trust in the news. In his gospel, John says, , "I have given them your word and the world has hated them, for they are not of the world any more than I am of the world. My prayer is not that you take them out of the world but that you protect them from the evil one. They are not of the world, even as I am not of it" (John, 17:14-16). No matter what is happening in the world around us we must trust and believe in God's word, that none of the evil impacts His believers. There are many scriptures in the bible that support God's promises to us.

We cannot quote the Word of God without believing it or it will not work.

As the summer was coming to a close, Rilee planned to return home for school and her birthday. I had a feeling that something great was about to happen; I just did not know what it could be. The enemy was trying his best to distract me from it because he was using people close to me to attack me, starting with my family. My grandmother Mama Woods was sick and we were told she could pass any day. There were things happening left and right that were beyond my control.

The day after my niece left, I met a guy that I absolutely loved. I won't mention his name because he was special to me. It was strange because a few years prior to moving to Houston, the Lord had given me a vision about a man who looked similar to him I was supposed to marry. He also looked exactly like the man on my vision board from 2019. This was the same year the Lord had given me the vision. We had so much in common and talked about alot of things. Anytime we hung out, we had such a great time. DeMarion liked him as well which was a plus. In fact, DeMarion liked this man so much that he would practically push me out the door to go spend time with him. Everyone in my circle including family loved him.

After all the horrible relationships I had been in, I wanted to make sure I was not wasting time on anyone who was not for me. I went on a fast right before I left to attend Faith Church Women's Conference in St. Louis. I yearned to be in God's presence and get the confirmation I needed and, because of the pandemic, my church in Houston was shut down. I knew that being at Faith Church St. Louis would give me the revive I needed.

While I was in St. Louis, I dropped off some balloons and cake to my grandmother because I missed her birthday. Due to COVID restrictions, I was unable to see her which made both of us sad. I couldn't hug her or see her smile. We had zoom meetings but it was not the same as in-person communication. The nurse offered to take a picture to give her with the cake and balloons to sit by her bed.

My trip was unforgettable; the conference was amazing, and I was so grateful to witness real women of faith come together to worship. I was tired of watching online and was not going to let COVID keep me from being in the house of the Lord. I had such a great time that I did not want to leave, but by the end of the conference I had the confirmation I needed. The Lord told me He needed to work on this man I was dating, but to trust in the Lord and not the relationship. I was not sure if God was inquiring about working on him now or working on him in the future; so I just let things play out.

When I got back to Houston we became closer. He would go through my notes for the videos I was doing to make sure the message was coming across effectively. He reviewed the previous ones I did and gave me key pointers or tips for improvement. He also inspired me to start my non-profit, Faith over Fear Transition Center Inc. I remember sitting on his couch and we were talking about things we wanted to do in the future. I told him that I wanted to create a transition center to help the homeless get off the street permanently and transition back into society. He turned to me and said, "Brittney, what are you waiting on and why haven't you started?" He went out with me one evening with another couple to help feed the homeless and support the vision. It was a phenomenal experience for the both of us. We discussed how the organization would bring impact to the community.

I was always afraid of the paperwork to start a business, which was one of my biggest reasons for never getting started. However, when he asked me why I hadn't already begun, a light bulb came on and I started immediately. The original name of the Transition Center was supposed to be Faith, Love & Hope

Transition Center, based on 1 Corithians, but the name was taken. I was working an upcoming outreach project with some other church members. We titled the project "Faith over Fear" and I decided that would be the perfect name for the business. My friend Lonneka connected me with a lady to help me get started, and then I connected with another person to work on my logo.

After all these years of talking about it, things were finally coming together. I was rapidly seeing the Lord's vision come to pass. I remember during that summer I kept saying in my videos that the Lord was doing things suddenly, and sure enough, he built Faith over Fear Transition Center suddenly.

I finally felt like things were moving in the right direction for me but a few weeks later, my boyfriend and I hit a bump in the road. We had a misunderstanding about the way I communicated something to him, and instead of picking up the phone to seek clarity, he decided to pull away, which made things worse. Communication is an essential key in any kind of relationship; in order to be successful at anything effective communication is a requirement. This is to ensure that any message is conveyed appropriately to the other party to eliminate any misunderstandings. A week later he finally got around to communicating verbally and he decided to walk away from our relationship. He tried to explain the timing wasn't right for him, but by then it was already too late and I was not listening.

This breakup was very emotional because three days later my great-grandmother Mama Woods passed away. My great-grandmother and I were really close. I considered her as a grandmother not great-grandmother; she told me I was one of her favorite grandchildren. She always worried about me finding the right man and would tell me every time I saw or spoke with her that he was coming. This all caught me by surprise. I was not expecting any of this to happen the way it did. I was a complete wreck and I did not have my man to give me the comfort I needed during this time. I had no one to comfort me and I felt so alone. It was as if I was grieving the loss of two people at the same time, and I fell into a slight depression. I did not want to go anywhere or do anything because all I could see was defeat. I felt like a heavyweight boxing champ that just got knocked out. Thank God for Ms.Denita, she was a blessing to my life and DeMarion's since the day we moved to Houston. Ms. Denita came over immediately and sat with me through my troubles, determined not to let me fall.

Troubles and pain will come but it is only temporary. Pain teaches us to lean on God and realize He is still in control. The loss of something is always a gain to something else. When a woman gives birth to a baby she always experiences contractions before the delivery. The contractions are painful and are generally signs that the baby is ready to come. The loss of my relationship and the unfortunate loss of my grandmother were the contractions I experienced to give birth to my vision. Giving birth is painful because you experience physical and emotional exhaustion. However, in the end, you gain a beautiful bundle of joy. In that moment I may have felt like I lost a lot but it helped me mature and develop for what was next. We don't know the plans God has for us, nor do we know the moment when He will say it's our time. We must be in preparation in and out of season so that when He tells us it's time to move we are not caught off guard.

When I returned to Houston after my grandmother's funeral, an awakening came over me and I began putting all my energy into my vision. I went out to serve with the couple I normally went out with on Thursday nights. We started praying with a man who was recently released from prison. He wanted to get his life in order to get his daughter back. A peace came over me knowing

I was headed in the right direction and Faith over Fear Transition Center was necessary. I remained committed to the vision despite what was happening around me, and again, doors began to open out of nowhere. The website was completed within a few weeks and I started receiving donations from so many people who believed in my vision. Opposition can never stop God, one touch of His favor can set you up for a lifetime.

Faith over Fear Transition Center completed three outreaches in the last months of the year and all of them were huge successes. God started connecting me with people who would help grow the ministry. His power was really behind the movement of this organization.

DeMarion was doing well with basketball and decided to start his own clothing line, "DM27". We stepped out on faith and began moving on it, unsure how it was going to turn out. The end goal was to teach him how to generate wealth for himself at a young age, preparing him for college. I am certain I will experience turbulence but it won't keep me from finishing the race.

I began writing this book to inspire others, to help them understand that no matter what you face in life, God can use you and can do anything through you. I always wanted to write a book and never got around to it. I believe that many people can relate to the things I have been through and use it as a driving force to go after their dreams. The pandemic may have looked like adversity to some, but for me it was a pathway to success.

Pastor David Crank declared earlier in the year during his 2020 revival that there would be a transfer of wealth this year and he most certainly did not lie. Wealth has transferred into my hands in a matter of months and I give all the credit to God. He did things I would have never been able to do with my own strength. He made impossible situations possible. 2020 may have started rough, but it ended very well for me.

I traveled many times in 2020, ending the year going to Atlanta, FLorida, St. Louis, and, finally, Dallas. It was only a few years ago that I could barely take a trip up the street. I am not telling you this to boast, but to help you truly see that God has been faithful to me and the same thing can happen for you. Circumstances do not have to be perfect to go after your dreams; you just have to be willing. When you have the faith that God can do anything, He will do everything. He will take you from the back of the line to the front of the line; He will open doors that no one can shut. I am so grateful to serve a God who never fails. He did not create you to exist but to live in divine purpose.

2021 began differently. I was completely distracted. Normally I start the new year with a vision board and go on a fast. Well, I was far from doing any of those things because of the distractions that occurred. I made some unwise decisions the first week into the new year when I should have been fasting and praying. I kept trying to start my fast then messing up and pushing the start date back. The enemy sees the plans that God has for your life and if the enemy can't take you out, he will distract you. I really had to have a pep talk with myself and God to get back on track.

When I returned from Dallas, I was determined to remain committed to my fast and let nothing stand in my way. I started out doing really well but about four days in, I got a call with some bad news and attempted to commit suicide. Even though the person delivering the message wanted me to understand it was not that bad, I perceived the news a completely different way. I sent my manager a message and told her I couldn't do this anymore and logged off.

I was crying hysterically and the devil whispered in my ear, "You might as well just kill yourself because no one needs you." I confess that I agreed with the devil and I started writing my son a goodbye letter. I told him how sorry I was, that I wasn't the mom he thought I was. I told him that someone would come to take good care of him.

I went into my bathroom and grabbed some pills and water. The minute I put the pills in my mouth the Lord yelled, "Brittney Stop! You are more than a conqueror, don't you trust me? How can I be an overcomer if you don't face adversity? How can I be a healer if I don't make you sick? How can I provide financial miracle if you did not go through a financial crisis? So no matter what they said, you have to trust me through it all." The moment the Lord stopped speaking, my best friend Lionel called me because he knew something was wrong. When I told him what was happening, he started speaking positivity over me saying, "You are stronger than that and you have so much to live for. Your son and so many people need you. Don't let the devil get you because it could be worse." I could tell from the sound of his voice that he was in tears. After all, what do you tell a person who has always been strong for others? He continued to talk me through this dark moment until I felt better. Then, to my surprise, my manager texted me, "Brittney, I am not sure what you are going through, but I do know you're a fighter and you're stronger than this. It may be a moment of weakness but remember how strong you are. I will pray for you as well." To ensure I was doing ok she told me to take the rest of the day off to take care of myself.

In those moments of darkness, God pulled me out and made sure I did not drown. The Lord spoke life into me, letting me know I was not alone and He was still with me. He used the right people at the right time to stop the plan of the devil. The moment I walked into 2021, the devil was fighting hard to ensure I didn't go after what God was trying to do in my life.

Every person has encountered an attack —Christian or non-Christian. Moments of attack does not mean defeat, they just teach us to really lean on God. It is so important to stay in prayer every second and every hour because the enemy is working day and night to try to take you out. The gospel of John tells us that, "The thief comes only to steal and kill and destroy. I came that they may have life and have it abundantly" (John, 10:10). The pandemic has tried to alienate us from each other and get us alone so the devil has the opportunity to attack our minds. Many people are dying from suicide and homicide because of the attack on our minds. Our mind is our greatest asset and we must protect it at all costs. If you think about something long enough, it begins to manifest. I am sharing this because I know many people have dealt with suicidal thoughts. The Lord loves you and is always with you. Don't ever feel like you have to be alone; connect with some accountability partners that are determined to never let you fall.

From that moment forward, I took back my life and remained focused on the vision. A few days later my son and I finally finished our vision boards. It took discipline, strength, revival, courage, dedication, and focus. The dictionary defines discipline "to train or develop by instruction and exercise, especially in self-control" ("discipline"). I had to discipline my mind to believe that "I can do all things through Christ who strengthens me" (Phillipians, 4:13). I had to remember I serve a God that will never give up on me.

It takes real discipline, strength, and dedication mixed with faith to accomplish your goals. You have to truly be committed to your purpose and run through the turbulence of life. God has created everyone on this earth with a unique purpose and it's up to us to get started. The first requirement is to believe in Him and then step out on faith to accomplish your dreams. God is not a man that He should lie, nor is He a God who has limitations. He is the same God who can heal you from COVID, the same God who can cover you when you leave your home, the same God who can bless your finances, and the same God who can do anything and everything. If you believe him for one thing, what will it cost you to believe Him for the rest? In the gospel of Matthew, we are reminded that "When he had gone indoors, the blind men came to him, and he asked them, 'Do you believe that I am able to do this?' 'Yes, Lord,' they replied" (Matthew, 9:28). I am a living witness to tell you that all it takes is your belief and trust in Him. Belief and action are the keys you need to take you from fear to faith.

CONCLUSION

Life has a way of teaching you things that you don't realize it is preparing you for your future. We don't get to choose the cards we were dealt, but we get to choose how to play the hand. We can't focus on the why; rather we have to keep our eyes focused on the who. We will forever be a student, always learning. Life is the university, and we are just preparing for the test. Even if we fail the test, we can't quit. We have to keep taking it until we pass.

There are no instructions on being a parent or whoever you are created to be. We are all new to what we are doing and we won't always get it right so we have to keep on learning. I don't claim to have mastered it all as I am still trying to strive to be the best version of myself I was created to be. I have made so many mistakes and bad choices along the way. In those mistakes I learned on whom to keep my focus. I went from my car being repossessed to my car being paid in full, from barely being able to afford groceries to having more than enough. You can't tell me that what God did for me He won't do for you as well.

I would not be the woman I am today without God. Even when you don't see anything happening keep believing. Even when you have to take a step back, still believe. I hope that you can walk away from this inspired, fully recharged and prepared to go after your dreams. In this season, you don't have to be who others want you to be. Instead, be who God has made you to be. Sometimes, in being who you were created to be, you won't look like everyone else. When you are chosen you are set apart. You are not average or mediocre but different; set apart to make a difference in this world.. Going after purpose will be challenging but if you give it all you have and all you are, it will be worth it in the end. Don't wait until you got it all figured out because while you are figuring it out God is working it out. The time is now to step into your future with boldness and fullness of joy. Never stop fighting and never stop believing in your dreams. No matter the circumstance, good or bad, keep pushing and keep the faith. I believe in you and can't wait to see you come forth like the star you were destined to be.

PRAYER OF ENCOURAGEMENT

Dear Heavenly Father,

I thank you for all that you have done and you are about to do in our lives. I thank you for being an ever-present help in times of trouble. I thank you for being the great God that you are. I thank you for being the comforter, the healer, the waymaker, the provider, and the protector. Lord, we lift Your name on high and we say thank you for all that You have done. If You choose not to do anything else, we are truly grateful for what You have already done.

Lord, I pray that each and every person who has read this book will go after their dreams, visions, or plans that are in alignment with your will. I pray they walk in power and with authority to speak those things into existence. I pray that you put a hedge of protection around them, that any weapon that tries to form against them will not prosper. I pray that you give them wisdom to make the right decisions in this season, hope in times of despair and peace that surpasses their understanding. Humble them to a place where their hearts are filled with gratitude. Don't allow them to be overcome by adversity but learn to trust in you through it all. Only allow positive words to come out of their mouths, rebuking any negative attack or comment that comes their way. Increase their faith to believe on another level and increase their finances to do the work of the Kingdom. I pray they are the head and not the tail, always above and never beneath. I pray that bondage and generational curses are broken from their lives and anything they put their hands to will prosper and succeed. Let your will be done in their lives. We declare these things to be so and so it will be.

In Jesus' Name, amen

WRITE THE VISION

I challenge you to write down three things you expect God to do for you this year. Include a scripture with it and the date of expectancy. Pray over it and I guarantee God will move.

    Then the LORD said to me, "Write my answer plainly on tablets, so that a runner can carry the correct message to others. This vision is for a future time. It describes the end, and it will be fulfilled. If it seems slow in coming, wait patiently, for it will surely take place. It will not be delayed (Habakkuk, 2:2-3).

1. _____

_____

Scripture: _____

Date of Expectation: _____

2. _____

_____

Scripture: _____

Date of Expectation: _____

3. _____

_____

Scripture: _____

Date of Expectation: _____

ABOUT THE AUTHOR

Brittney Kendle was born and raised in St.Louis, MO, where she encountered most of her challenges and found her faith. She has always had a will to give and inspire others, and to teach her son to be an inspiration using his talent. She would always journal her experiences and talk about combining them into a book. She has served in homeless communities for many years and has a heart for those in need. She relocated to Houston in 2019 where she discovered her purpose. She is the founder of a non-profit, Faith over Fear Transition Center, Inc., where they are transitioning homeless individuals from the streets to live prosperously in society. She is the part owner with her son of new and upcoming DM27 Clothing, a brand created for her son to inspire others through clothing. Brittney also has a YouTube channel, Faith over Fear TC Podcast created to inspire others to willingly follow Christ. She is also the announcer for MDLTV and a host for the new and upcoming Freedom Room; a faith based digital talk show created to have conversations with no limits.

Brittney has a bachelor's degree in Health Management and plans to open up a health center in at-risk communities to provide them with healthcare. She is a devoted mother who puts everything she has into her son, DeMarion Morgan, to ensure he succeeds. She enjoys being a basketball mom and being her son's biggest cheerleader when he is on the court watching him grow as an athlete and teammate. She also enjoys being a favorite aunt to Rilee, Zyon and all her other nieces and nephews.

WORKS CITED

"Access Your Bible from Anywhere." BibleGateway.com: A Searchable Online Bible in over 150 Versions and 50 Languages., www.biblegateway.com/. Accessed January 29, 2021.

"Discipline." *Merriam-Webster.com Dictionary*, Merriam-Webster, https://www.merriam-webster.com/dictionary/discipline. Accessed 29 Jan. 2021.

From Fear To Faith

Made in the USA
Columbia, SC
20 June 2021